The sound of beautiful music
creeps softly into the heart;
rhapsody ensues.

~ *Candice James*

Also by Candice James

Behind The One-Way Mirror (Silver Bow) 2022
Double Trouble Vol III – poemetrics (Silver Bow) 2022
Double Trouble Vol II – deviate the levitate (Silver Bow) 2021
Call of the Crow (Silver Bow Publishing) 2021
Double Trouble Vol I – poems from the edge(Silver Bow) 2020
The Path of Loneliness (Inanna Publications) 2020
Rithimus Aeternam (Silver Bow) 2019
The 13th Cusp ((Silver Bow) 2018
Short Shots (Silver Bow) 2017
City of Dreams (Silver Bow) 2016
The Water Poems (Ekstasis Editions) 2015
Purple Haze (Libros Libertad) 2014
A Silence of Echoes (Silver Bow) 2014
Merging Dimensions (Ekstasis Editions) 2013
Midnight Embers – sonnets (Libros Libertad) 2013
Ekphrasticism (Silver Bow) 2013
Colours of India (Xpress Publications) 2012
Shorelines – villanelles (Silver Bow) 2012
Bridges and Clouds (Silver Bow) 2011
Inner Heart a Journey (Silver Bow) 2010
A Split in the Water (Fiddlehead Poetry Books) 1979

The Depth
Of
The Dance

Candice James

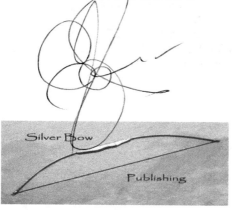

Silver Bow Publishing

Box 5 – 720 – 6th Street,
New Westminster, BC
V3C 3C5   CANADA

Title: The Depth Of The Dance
Author: Candice James
Cover Painting: "Dance Of The Butterflies" Candice James
Layout/Design: Candice James
Editing: Candice James

ISBN: 9781774032459
ISBN: 9781774032466
© 2022 Silver Bow Publishing

Library and Archives Canada Cataloguing in Publication

Title: The depth of the dance / Candice James.
Names: James, Candice, 1948- author.
Description: Poems.
Identifiers: Canadiana (print) 20220492557 | Canadiana (ebook) 20220492573 | ISBN 9781774032459
   (softcover) | ISBN 9781774032466 (Kindle)
Classification: LCC PS8569.A429 D47 2022 | DDC C811/.54—dc23

Dedication

To the musicians, dancers and lovers
who have filled my cup
to overflowing,

Contents

Cats & Jazz / 11
A Song Is A Song Is A Song / 12
Angels Sang / 13
Blue Rhapsody / 14
Choir / 15
Cool Water Piano Keys / 16
Cinematic / 17
Java Jazz / 19
Degrees Of Depth / 20
Midnight Sonatas / 21
Music Ceases / 22
Music Of The Hautboys Under The Stage / 23
Pump Up The Volume/ 24
Ruby Crowned Songs / 25
Rumbling Thunder / 26
Soft On My Heart / 27
The Blue Of A Fading Song / 28
The Edge Of The World / 29
The Edge / 31
The Emptiness / 32
Music, You And Me / 33
The Piano's Waxed Ebony Face / 34
The Rhythm Of The Universe Within / 36
The Song / 37
The Sound Of Shadows / 38
The Sweet Of The Wood /39
There Are Songs / 40
Thirsty Spirit / 41
Unsung / 42
Whispering Through The Blue / 43
Timing / 44
Shadow Dancers / 45
Poet's Dance / 46
Sonatastice Perpetuum / 47
Silent Songs And Rubber Bands / 48
Wisdom's Stone / 49
Guitar Breeze / 50
A Statue / 51

Dried Flowers Of Youth / 52
Dancing To A Memory / 53
Dead And Gone / 54
One Chord / 55
One Heartbeat Away / 56
Atmosphere And Rhythm / 57
Musical Magic / 58
The Birds Of Prey / 59
A Burnt-Out Torch Song / 60
Catchers In The Rye / 61
Deep Silver Silence Of Song / 62
The Heartbeat Of Existence / 63
Laying Soft Upon My Heart / 64
The Rhythm Of Romance / 65
Rounders / 66
Sparkle Of A Distant Star / 67
Days Of Old Gold / 68
The Strum / 69
To Visualize The Dream / 70
Water And Rain / 71
We'll Fly No More / 72
Hardened / 73
Heartache's Aftermath / 74
The Amber Glow / 75
Leading Me Home / 76
Leaving The Harbor / 77
Looking, Not Seeing / 78
Periwinkle Pond / 79
Phantom Moon / 80
The Crows And I / 81
The Dance / 82
The Song I Am / 83
Voices Of Yesterday / 84
White Swans At Midnight / 85
Home At Last / 86
Breath And Song / 87
Heartbeat Of The Stars / 88
I Sang You A Love Song / 89
Inside The Forest Of Song / 90
Piano Of Secrets / 91

Play The Rose For Me / 92
The Violin / 93
Thin Sleep / 94
We Danced / 96
Birds On A Wire / 97
A Statue / 98
Defining Moment / 99
Deep Gold Frost And Soft Silver Songs / 100
Dance With The Surprises / 101
Dancing In The Dark Alone / 102
Eulogenic / 103
Flamenco Fire Dance / 104
Fluid Silence / 105
Guitar Strings / 106
Justin Bieber And The Blue Petal Dream / 107
Night Shift / 108
No Trace / 109
Opposite Deficiencies / 110
Outside Heaven's Door / 111
I Promise You This / 112
Saturday's Wishes / 113
Sometimes I Dance / 114
The Dance (sestina) / 115
The Depth Of The Dance / 117
The Dreamer Of Dreams / 118
The Pink Velvet Room / 120
The Sands Of Eternity / 122
The Silence / 123
The Singer / 124
Inside Out / 125
Decibel Rhythm / 126
Disco Fever / 127
Deciphering The Code / 128
Replacements / 129
Music Spheres / 130
Rippling / 131
Fade Away / 132
Coda / 13
Mystic Moon / 134
Deep Blue Purple / 135

Deep In The Shadows / 136
Dockside At Midnight / 137
The Gathering Of The Trees / 138
The Gold Of That Moment / 139
In The Amber Glow / 140
Sea Of Regret / 141
Shuffle / 142
Summer In Your Hair / 143
The Waters of Sleep / 144
Time Interrupted / 145
Winter's Shadowland / 146
Beautiful Magic / 147
A Distant Moaning / 148
Forever ... Yet Never / 149
The Only Moment / 150
Raw Red Nightmare / 151
Tumbling Down / 152

Author Profile / 153

Cats & Jazz

The cat's in the cradle.
There's jazz in the cellar.
Blue notes purr softly
thickening the edge of emotion.

While the cat claws
its way into sleep's oblivion,
I dimensionalize
into the cellar sound,
the stellar sound.

I climb to the tip
of a raw red note;
then slide down the edge
of a baby blue chord:
       suspended,
       upended,
swaying to the riffs and groove
in the smooth of a satin beat.

The cow jumps over the moon.
The dish runs away with the spoon.

The music flows
then slowly ebbs
into the sands of time.
The revery dims,
dissolves.

      The cellar falls silent.

      The cat in the cradle
         falls asleep.

    The time for dreams is at hand.

A Song Is A Song Is A Song

There was music,
        hazy notes and beats,
                waiting a long time to be born.

        Waiting In the dark womb of time
                        to be illuminated
        by the spark of sound.

Then suddenly, within a wall of silence,
        a song comes alive
                and breaks through
to lead my sleeping heart
        onto a street of neon dreams
and a new way of dancing.

                And there you were
        singing and dancing passionately,
                without reservation.
        I fell under your spell
                mesmerized completely.
                        I loved the song you sang.

Then the notes and beats
        collided with the wall of silence
                and your voice faded away.

        Sometimes the tempo doesn't fit
        the mood of words and melody.

Sometimes a song is just a song.
Sometimes a song is more than a song.

                But always,
                always ...
        a song is a song is a song.

Angels Sang

Angels sang and circled our souls
          weaving us into the fabric
     of their eternal song.

We walked between two golden deer
     flanked by albino wolves.

Inside the oneness of our breath,
ravens and doves circled above:
living auras adorning our souls.

          We walked on the backlit side
               of a sacred silver moon
          inside the palm of God.

          Inside this surreal forest
     we held hands with the angel of death
and danced with the pale ghosts of the past
          as the music turned the pages of life
          writing us into eternity's symphony.

          Angels sang and circled our souls
               weaving us into the fabric
                    of their eternal song.

Blue Rhapsody (sonnet)

The ink and blood are mixed together now.
What is this inspiration turned to chill?
A buried heartache 'neath lust's rusted plow
where once it spun with love on passion's hill?
Where fevered brow did glisten with love's sweat?
The bluest rhapsody invades my mind
reverberating echoes of regret;
the final throes of love maligned and blind.
But should tomorrow bring new rhapsody
and fill my heart and lift it from the mire,
unwrapped in surrealistic poetry
I'll bathe in pools of inspiration's fire.

Then, once again I'll kiss, in moonlit tryst,
those lips, it seems forever, I have missed.

Choir

A bruised heartbeat turns into tones.
                    Vibrating, pulsating,
            emanating colours, electricity.
Magnetizing illusions to reality.
                Silence to sound.
                    Whispers to voices.
Cascading upward toward Nirvana,
            resting place of the pristine soul.

A slow-breathing, inspired sky
moistens its parted lips.
                Puffs its smooth cheeks.
                    Blows sweet inspiration
            trumpeting through time to the lead in.
Fading up into crescendos of white rhapsodies
            and opaque serenades,
                    it drifts and drives tenderly
            into the core of the choir.

        In the valley of eight echoes
        the choir arises and prepares:
        Stirring angelic powers.
        Awakening wings of glory.

Raw red notes shimmer and shine.
White pearls glisten and gleam.
Blue diamonds underscore the music.
Black stilettos beat out the rhythm of the universe.

Thunder reigns down from the throne
            and suddenly ...
                the choir sings.

Cool Water Piano Keys

The cool water piano keys
     feel solid;
  then ripple like magic.
The music begins to breathe
and flow like wet whispers
splashing onto the face of your mind.

    At first a faint whisper,
    becoming a rhapsody,
    fading into a torch song.

    Burnt embers,
     rough notes,
      wax full
in the moonglow of a sultry night
before endless winter blacks its light.

    Then,
the music feathers down,
cascades into a hard rain,
abrasive to the touch.

  Too brittle not to break.
    Too fragile,
    it shatters.

    The cool water piano keys
      turn to ice.

16

Cinematic

**(written to the music of the band Fusionstein
at Cavalcade of Merriment Vancouver, BC Nov 24, 2016)**

I am lost in a bizarre wedding bell of sound:
      chaos and destruction
      marrying my evil twins;
         and I ...
      I am the only uninvited guest.

With scissor-step precision,
      I mount a surreal cliff of clefs
         to ride the pinnacle
            of a sonic wave
            I've managed to catch
         in the curl of a reversing tidal bore
      where my other self is languishing lazily.

I am found latching onto a glory stone.
         I pyramid into the soak
            of a tsunami
        chasing musical notes
           that cannot be tamed;
          and I cannot be blamed
        for their wanton disobedience.

This sleepless garage band
      is somebody else's baby.
         so they can rock it.

Locked in the sweet sonorous pitch
      and neon glow
         of a moon-struck chord
          piercing the eye of midnight.
      rose petals and stardust
          whirl and swirl
         beneath the feet
     of nude opalescent dancers
         of the third kind.

The pale ghosts of yesterday
                    resurrected
            are coming alive
                    in film clips and audio bytes
            pulsating on a cutting room floor
                    of camera-ready lenses.

                    It's all so rhythmic
                            and
                    so very, very cinematic.

            Even the dance smiles.

Java Jazz (sonnet)

Those sparkling lusty nights at Java Jazz.
We slow danced close as Salve sang her soul;
and Eddie played the sweetest razzmatazz
as we held hands in amber candle glow.
And there we were reflecting in love's eyes,
the lovelight, music, dancing, and crab cakes.
Your heartbeat wove the fabric of my sighs
before you changed the pattern to heartaches.
But if I think on Java Jazz and you
those magic melodies tug at my heart;
then yesterday appears out of the blue.
I feel the same old thrill as at the start.

There are some memories even time can't kill.
I loved the way we were. I always will.

Degrees Of Depth

I wait

                    while
                      a
                    lonely
                    violin

                    whispers
                      softly
          through
                      the
                    shadows.

You approach
    and
suddenly

                    the world
                      is a
                    symphony.

Midnight Sonatas
(Villanelle)

I dipped my pen into the Milky Way.
It painted symphonies across the sky
and then I heard midnight sonatas play.
An angel waking up began to sway
so with a second look and sweeping sigh
I dipped my pen into the Milky Way.
It lit the night and drowned out all the gray.
On sacred sound my soul began to fly
and then I heard midnight sonatas play.
What once had been chaotic disarray
began to shed its mask and torn disguise.
I dipped my pen into the Milky Way.
It painted a new face inside the fray
with smiles of silk and bright blue blazing eyes
and then I heard midnight sonatas play.
The universe wept and knelt down to pray
as teardrops built and then fell from my eyes.
I dipped my pen into the Milky Way
and then I heard midnight sonatas play.

Music Ceases

The music ascends,
            coils, bends and blends
                    in colours and tones;
            and explodes
      into an operatic ocean
            of vibrant sight and sound.

In the hills and valleys
            of this tidal symphony
                waves dance:
              rolling and rocking,
              walking and talking,
                chasing and stalking,
            pirouetting, prancing
            and shadow dancing.

          Romancing the coveted opus stone
              hidden beneath the sea.

          Then suddenly,
the eye in the sky's viscosity unveils.
          Sounds of sadness slowly evolve;
              then fade and dissolve.

The weary waves are falling ...
              falling asleep.

The symphony ebbs,
                recedes and drowns
              in reverberating waves.

                And then ...
            the music ceases.

Music Of The Hautboys Under The Stage
written to the painting by Jack Rootman
"MUSIC OF THE HAUTBOYS UNDER THE STAGE"

The haunting sounds from beneath a surreal ocean
    rise to the stage of the waves:
to drift across a fading Monet sky,
    splashing cool water and stardust
    onto the weary moon's face,
      awakening her
    to the echo of burgeoning sound-rise.

She opens her evanescent eye,
peeks over a silent mountain,
    and sits in rapt audience
      listening intently
    to the whiskey-wet whispers,
      mystic slurs and audio radiance
        vibrating and resonating
      in glorious magnificence
    across a vast expanse of sea and sky.

A tidal wind
    and underwater current
      sweep over bone and reed
        creating a watery drift
        of soft melodrama and mood,
          ebbing and flowing
        in frequency and wave
      from shoormal to shore.

The music of the night
      resounds.

    The concert in the deep
      reverberates
    with the music of the hautboys
      under the stage.

Pump Up The Volume

Pump up the volume.
       Pump up the volume!

The music flows,
       balancing on the raw red edges
              of stiletto sharp notes,
       sliding down the slippery jagged blades
              of suspended chords.

I cut them with the knives of my mind
       into little chunks
              of multi coloured glass
       that scratch at my spirit
              vibrating in rainbow tones.
Drums keep beating;
       hollowed out bones
         on wet deerskin,
     smacking rhythm into my soul.

       Rasping roars.
Pounding pulsations.
       Pistol whipped frenzy
              oozing frequencies,
       piercing pierced ears
              with numbing needles of noise.

Tripping on stones and tones,
       stumbling through infinity
              I emerge:
       Misty flavoured.
              Dripping with honey.
       Whispering whisky wet kisses
              into every heartbeat.

Pump up the volume!

       Pump up the volume,
              ... until I am the music.

Ruby Crowned Songs

I talk to the slick black pavement
      in ruby-crowned songs
tuning the air to a fevered pitch.

      Even the sky sweats.

Beads of warm summer rain
fall into my outstretched palms
      as I dance
down life's highway of dreams.

I throw myself
into the river of night
      and dream a wild beat
      onto rain-streaked mirrors.

A pale moon glistens,
high in the sky,
      as I two-step toward
      the croon of the night
and the satin whisper
of ruby crowned songs.

The bite sized stars:
      Twinkle and gleam.
      Dive into my eyes.
      Slide down my throat.

With a breath and a shiver
      I exit the river
         to shine the face
of this dream I'm dreaming.

Singing a brand-new ruby-crowned song,
      I shimmy and jive
      through a sky of wonder.
      to the beckoning beat
      of distant drums.

Rumbling Thunder
(written to the music of the band Fusionstein
at Cavalcade of Merriment event at 7 Lounge, Vancouver, BC 2016)

Shimmering candlelight
          illuminating flickering paintings
    on the backlit side of a trembling tear.

This image:
      a modern day Monet caricature
    of an old destroyed world is resurrected...
        and someone is speaking
  in a broken and hackneyed language,
  with bits and pieces of scarred skin
      accentuating the scene.

Inside, it is outside in.
Outside, it is locked inside
      its own brittle cold
      that burns a frost of cares.

There is a silvering to this moment in time;
    a glossing-over of an old dusty rhyme;

      And all the while
  the candlelight continues shimmering.

  The paintings continue flickering.

  The wall shimmies and shakes,
    into quick staccato steps
    dancing stealthily
  up the down staircase of dreams.

Shiny ribbons of music
    stumble and crumble
      in an evening reign
    of ebony lightning
    and the deafening silence
    of rumbling, thunderous song.

Soft On My Heart

November, a rain soaked city,
the asphalt slick and glossy
trying to shine the day.
A song from yesterday permeates the air
as we travel toward the ocean
in search of our long lost summer.

Your teardrops fall soft on my heart.

We're caught in this eternal winter
strumming our heart strings,
trying to give our song new wings.

Twilight shadows increase
and threaten as we journey
toward our separate perditions.

I softly tighten my embrace
to ease your sorrow.

Love's spine cracks.
Our string breaks.
We go our separate ways.

The sky darkens.
The music dies.
But still,
the song lingers on.

Your teardrops fall soft on my heart.

Forever ...
soft on my heart.

The Blue Of A Fading Song

Trapped in the blue of a fading song
another long night lingers on:
The music and the dancers gone.
I'm lost on a street of shattered dreams,
unraveling night at its tattered seams,
searching for an ember or spark
to light my way out of this dark.

Then a sudden moon rises high above.
Little stars sparkle like bright eyes in love.
Twilight flexes its fingers and reach
enshrouding an empty, desolate beach.
A seagull's cry slices the sky.
An errant teardrop falls from my eye.

Trapped in the blue of a fading song,
with notes and chords that don't belong,
I stand at the edge of a broken seaside
bathed in mystery and moonlight
searching for you and yesterday
and distant dreams so far away.

Another long night lingers on.
The music and the dancers gone.
They've disappeared into the dawn.

But I remain ...
trapped in the blue of a fading song.

The Edge Of The World

The music shakes, spills,
falls off the edge of the world
in muted tones and keys.

Moments slow, stop,
        collapse
    into the eternal now.

                Time ceases to exist.

            Inside this vacuum:
                    Silence within.
                    Silence without.

In this still, small space,
            I move as wet hard mist
        splashing, splintering, scattering
                above myself,
                below myself
                    and yet,
                within myself.

        I peer through
        a surreal foggy lens
        at nondescript ghosts
        moving their lips
        in deafening silence.

I perceive a whisper of wings,
a flutter of heartbeats.

            Inside this vacuum:
                    Silence within.
                    Silence without.

So, I

      f

          a

             l

                l

off the edge of the world
in muted tones and keys
into a silence of echoes;
then rise
in major 7th chords:

A suspended song ...
slowly ...
slowly
becoming a symphony
of beautiful heavenly sound.

The Edge

I'm at the edge
of beautiful music
I can't quite hear;
  at the base
  of a new knowledge
  I can't quite grasp.

I'm looking at a masterpiece
I can't see clearly.
The colours dance
and shape-shift through each other
  to an indistinct beat
  that ebbs and flows
  inside its fluid flux.

A ring of fire,
I flicker and flare
in embers and flames
trying to turn
  diamonds to dust,
  gold to water,
  and silver to black onyx notes.

  I'm at the edge
of the most beautiful music,
  grasping at notes
  just out of reach,
trying to find the key to my song.

31

The Emptiness

Emptiness falls through the trees,
creeps through the grass,
climbs through my window and embraces me.
It bruises my lips,
lays heavy on my heart.

     Once there used to be music.
     Now there is only emptiness.

Darkness undresses
in a lonely night's dream
and a dreamy night's loneliness.
Twilight's shuffle is indistinct, muffled.
     Like cards dropped on a carpet.
     Like tiny cardboard houses
     collapsing in whispers.

In the distance a hollow bell rings,
     fades to silence.

I know there is music somewhere,
     but here ...
here the emptiness deafens.

Music, You And Me

The music was so beautiful.
It was love and so were we,
spirits sewn together
soul deep in eternity.

We thought we were inseparable
but time and life got in the way.
Dreams became irreparable
inside our sad and tragic play.

Somewhere down the road of time
we'll find our long lost sunshine.
We'll make sweet music again
and move back into 'then':
> When we kept each other alive.
> When days were etched in gold.
> We found a way to survive
> but couldn't keep out the cold.

> Even so,
the music still plays on;
although the song's forgotten
and yesterday is gone.

But no matter what
it will always be:
music, you and me
throughout eternity.

> Music, you and me
> throughout eternity.

The Piano's Waxed Ebony Face

A freeze frame flash of death and her daughter,
        dancing to a haunting melody,
appeared incognito behind a backlit neon cloud
and lit up a steeplechase race of phantom horses
        chasing a thousand dreams
        down millions of miles
    of static wires and telephone lines
        strung on the whispers of time.
    Buzzing and buzzing, on and off,
        on a lonely, deserted highway.

A lost angel rode on the wings of an eagle
carrying a dead crow to the wake of wild things.
A horseless halter and broken bridle
fell from the tombstones of time
and the universe was dancing with death
        to the sound of a cracked digeridoo
        in a woodwind band of bass relief.

In the cradle cap crown of a broken sky
an antique piano was lowered
from a twenty second floor penthouse parlor.

    Ghostly fingers, in white satin gloves,
        were tapping ... tap, tap, tapping.
Tapping that haunting melody, over and over again.

There was a shiny silver basket
and glossy antique porcelain firedogs
precariously balanced
on the piano's waxed ebony face.

There was an aficionado
waxing his moustache
while playing a tune with his toes
and drinking red wine and roses
from a stained glass crystallized goblet
dusted with baby's breath and snowflakes.

34

An image of a derelict sailboat
appeared on his forehead
and the wings of a dying dove
fluttered, fluttered, fluttered then fell
onto a faded Monet masterpiece
that had seen better days in the war.

With his left hand bouncing
back and forth on the ivories and ebonies
his right hand kept perfect time
twirling and waxing his moustache;
    and all the while his lover
was lying dead in a four-poster bed
on the deadly twenty-second floor
with a stone above her head
and blood-stained sheets beneath her body.

All these images were only props
in a freeze frame flash of death and her daughter
as they slowly stepped out
from behind the backlit neon cloud
and basked in the shine
of the piano's waxed ebony face
and the gaze of an dead audience.

They smiled as if they were alive
and bowed gracefully again and again
to the deafening sound of one hand clapping
in the land of haunting melodies
    at the edge of the living dead.

    And
the piano's waxed ebony face
    smiled ...

    in moot appreciation.

The Rhythm Of The Universe Within

A hard rain claws at her eyes
and tears at her ears.
in this invisible forest she's dancing through.
The melodies are timeless and torn.
     The rhythm of the universe within
        ... sighs.

No one is foolish enough
to venture this far into oblivion,
this far into a blank universe
that can't be imprinted.
The hard, icy, stiletto rain
     continues falling.
It echoes with her breath only.
     The rhythm of the universe within
        ... cries.

The melodies have lost their soft edges.
     They're dissolving into
stumbling notes and broken chords,
unaware of the key they were written in.
They have transmuted themselves
into living breathing metronomes .
     Timeless and torn.
     Old and worn.
The hard rain continues its journey
in whispers she can no longer decipher.
     The rhythm of the universe within
        ... dies.

She can't dance anymore
inside this crumbling steeple.

    She's lost herself
       and
she's lost the rhythm of the universe within.

     She cries.

The Song

You walk in dark shadows
at the edge of night
and softly climb into my dreams;
and then the music starts.

We slow dance
through the notes,
writing love letters on suspended chords
as we tap our way into each other.

There is a silence of voices throughout
as we search to find the lyrics that define us;
side-stepping toward the keys we lost.

     As we grasp for them
     they dissolve at our touch.

Forever lost to each other now,
you fade into the dark shadows
at the edge of night,
climb out of my dreams
and the music stops.

     I cling to the silence
       seeking solace,
trying desperately to remember the song ...
       knowing full well
      I won't be able to.

The Sound Of Shadows

In the sound of shadows
circular haloes extend themselves,
through hollow nights
and non-descript days,
chewing on sunbeams and moonglow.
      exhaling mist and fog
  into my already dampened spirit.

In the sound of shadows
there is no music, no cadence,
only a haunting hum of whispers
      I don't want to hear.

But they grow louder,
clawing incessantly
with long bony fingers
at a memory that lingers:
slicing my mind into reality,
peppering my heart with sighs and lies,
spilling onto the mirrors of my soul,
resurrecting images
better left dead.

In the sound of shadows
I hear everything
except my own voice.

The Sweet Of The Wood

The player owns the stage:
white leather shoes
and a blue guitar,
grooving the beat
in the mood of the moment.

    The notes fly high:
uncaged ravens of the night,
weaving a web of excitement.

Supple, staccato fingers
    gliding ,like silk.
on the barb of steel wound strings,
pulling off and slapping on,
coaxing the depth of sound
from within the sweet of the wood.

The sound reverberates,
stirring the night into mellow echoes,
    vibrant excitement,
    and easy living.

Expounding the sweet of the wood,
    wrapping the mood
    In rainbow strings...
    the player,
    a blue guitar
    and a touch of silk
breathe the music alive.

There Are Songs (sonnet)

I wave goodbye to urchins from my past.
They squeal with great delight as I depart,
but there are tear filled ghosts before the mast
lamenting my departure with sad heart.
Breathe deep and keep the weeping minimal
and hidden from the wild and woolly throngs.
As I drift at the edge of Autumn's fall
I hum forgotten yet familiar songs
vibrating softly on a stranger's lips.
I can`t quite grasp their names from memory.
It's almost there and then its essence slips,
into the yesterdays of you and me.

Yes there are songs, and there are songs sung blue,
but none so sweet as those I sang with you.

Thirsty Spirit
**(written to the music of the band Fusionstein
at 7 Lounge event, Vancouver, BC Nov 24, 2016)**

I'm riding down a derelict breeze
            where music feeds my need.
I was hiding
        Inside a wrinkled pocket of sand
            in my mind
        before this wind found me.
        and pushed me through
            living technicolor doors
        with exquisite waterproof eyelashes...
            opening and closing
        in exacting rhythm
            and perfect harmony

I am thirsty
        for the wet of a water song
            the dry of a desert song
        the cool of a winter song
            and the heat of a summer song.

Electric fingertips play a ragtime piano
        and flaccid wrists strum a broken ukulele
            with an elastic pick
        shaped like a tiny running shoe.

Alive with static shockproof laces
            and rubber band music
        the songs become cloaked
        in glorious sequined melodies
            that turn into neon smiles
        whispering coveted words of wisdom.

The stage becomes wet with stumbling wonder
            flowing like satin wine
        into my thirsty spirit
            bringing my soul alive ...
                Rock on!!.

Unsung

I sing the nameless song
with unsung lyrics.

I walk down a street
of long shadows.
Artifacts of a broken sun
held in the echo of wet moon
pound the pavement
in the canyons of my mind.

I take repast
at a table suspended in the air.
Read the invisible menu.
Digest the transient nourishment
in a silent ocean
that has no shorelines.

I lay in a bed of quantum dreams,
surrounded by slices of time
rotating in surreal dimensions
of yin and yang whispers,
wet to the touch
yet dry as a desert bone.

I sing the nameless song
with unsung lyrics,
slingshot past sun, moon and stars
into the tranquil pause between heartbeats.

In tune with the universe.
I am the nameless song.
I am the unsung lyrics.

      I wait ...
for my song to be born.

Whispering Through The Blue
(Tribute for Rex Howard 1930-2012)

In serenades and ballads
your memory lingers on,
whispering through the blue
of a fading song.
> If I listen I can hear you
> singing soft and low,
> star-dusted melodies
> in twilight's afterglow.

The sweet of the steel.
Guitar riffs and strums.
The groove of the bass.
The beat of the drums.
> The sweet, salty, powdered,
> sugar dreams of yesterday,
> tug gently at my heart strings
> and then I drift away.

If I close my eyes
I can still hear you play
those old favorite songs,
that familiar swing and sway.
> I hear your voice echoing
> in shadows of the rain.
> The sparkle and shine
> of your music's refrain;

In serenades and ballads
your memory lingers on,
whispering through the blue
of a fading song.

> Whispering through the blue
> of a fading song.

Timing

All great music and song
has fabulous melody, lyric and rhythm.
And, most importantly,
        perfect, exquisite, beautiful
                timing.

All great happenings in life
are contingent upon rhythms melding and fitting.

        The beat of your heart
        is the groove of my soul.

Finally I'm in step with myself.

        Step aside for no one.
        For no man.
        No matter how great the threat.

        Dance to only my music.
          Timing is everything
        unto the rhythm of love.

Dance my dreams
    to a higher dimension.

        You are the higher dimension of me
            and I am striving to climb into you,
                so I can climb back into myself.

Shadow Dancers

We shared precious slices of time,
cold drinks, hot jazz and poetic rhyme,
locked in a burning question
searching for the elusive answer
indelibly marked and branded
each other's shadow dancer.

On a slice of time we danced into the lights;
Nirvana nights, and gossamer flights
wrapped in the warp of a Rorschach ink stain
to the edge of a dream and back again.

  In the shadow dance
  of our brief romance
  our slices of time
  began to unwind.

In seductive pantomime
and a haze of whiskey and wine
our brief romance ran out of time,
flickered and faded and then flat-lined.

  . Like fine champagne
  left out in the rain
  the bubbles burst
  and the kick disbursed.

   Now ...
firmly ensconced in eternity's flame,
helpless pawns in destiny's game,
on the wheel of karma we rock'n'roll
burnt into the edge of each other's soul;
  eternally marked and branded
  each other's shadow dancer.

Poets' Dance

Hazy circles of possibilities
vibrate and float haphazardly touching down,
onto the jagged squares of quiet desperation,
in deafening silence without a sound.

Inside this massive silence,
that holds all the answers ,
we remain the unanswered questions;
the pantomime dancers.

All things pass away; then come to pass again.

Do not wait to step into the sunshine of your soul;
the best part of you is beckoning you to open the scroll.
So, step into the sacred circle of the poets' dance
where quicksilver lightning blends dreams with romance
shaking the spirit's eternal foundations
and rocking the cradle of great expectations.

It keeps spinning toward you, that wheel of fate,
waiting for you to step up to the plate.
Your hopes and your dreams are agleam in the sun,
so, pick up the bat and hit that home run.

Follow the path of quills and ink stains.
Follow your heart with every breath
and engrave the surreal letters of life
onto the well-worn parchment of death.

All things pass away; then come to pass again.

We are all searching for the God particle,
quite unaware that 'we' are the God particle.

The answers you seek aren't found in the vast expanse.
        Look inward angel ...
                        step into the poets' dance!

Sonatastice Perpetuum

A ribbon of hard sound reverberates
in my reverie; it shakes and wakes
a parlour of numb nerves, a long time asleep,
into a brand-new world that can't weep.

I witness blue music climbing green mountains
to find a lost glade of pristine fountains.
Born from the deepest scar on despair's face,
a raincloud scales a luminous staircase
that blinds the frail and frivolous eye
sewing it shut so it can't cry.

I'm reborn and baptized in sleek symphonies
of glorious sound and sweet mysteries,
with ear-piercing highs and heart wrenching lows.
It's all moving too fast and then it slows.
I lose control and my bearings once more
while searching in vain for Nirvana's lost score
hiding behind a blue bubble door.

I wallow half frozen in quicksand's mire.
My matches are wet and I can't light a fire.
At the core of this tinder-box dry rot forest
dead birds are singing an out of tune chorus;
and the Lord of the Flies is the crazed composer
conducting this bizarre operatic exposure
played on a cracked didgeridoo,
turning you into me and me into you
in a scotch and soda watered down score;
and I just can't take this bliss anymore.

It's too beautiful to listen to and remain sane.
Borne of never-ending relentless rain
and divine despair's greatest living pain:
sonatastice perpetuum again and again,
now ad infinitum for the insane.

Silent Songs And Rubber Bands

Within the glaring truth of blurred reality
penury and punishments pass by fleetingly;
and breath and death dance hand in hand
to silent songs and rubber bands.

Above the rolling thunderclouds
where rainbows are conceived,
beneath a tattered sky I stood and suddenly believed
a billion less a billion stars leaves nothing, only mist;
and as I peered into the mist I saw in ghostly tryst:
Heaven's angels chanting songs of love and sanctity
leading broken spirit souls into eternity.

Embraced by loving arms,
  held in an angel's sway
    swiftly from life's raw nightmare
    I was swept away

A sinner, now repented, I shed my soiled clothes,
and like a newborn phoenix, slowly I arose,
to dance to silent songs in resurrection's hall;
then suddenly without warning I heard a distant call.
A fluttering of angel's wings within a gathering throng
loosed the breath of heaven into a sacred song.

And then the sky ripped open,
        with her golden gates flung wide,
and all God's chosen children were escorted inside.

And I ... I was amazed I was resting in God's palm,
safe forever from life's storms at peace within his calm

Inside heaven's domain I dance in mercy's glow
to silent songs and rubber bands and I have come to know
that breath and death walk hand in hand
and are the kindred souls
beating God's eternal drum when the thunder rolls.

48

Wisdom's Stone (sonnet)

So tired of hiding under wisdom's stone
I cast my fate onto a wild west wind.
Old hobos gathered round and set the tone,
reciting stories they could not rescind.
I spied from the left corner of my eye
a homeless beggar clothed in dreams of gold.
The dreamer of my dream was passing by;
he offered me a story I could hold.
My palm pulsated with the written word
and sparkling diamonds spilled from polished coal
In poetry and songs I'd never heard,
imploding rapture deep within my soul.

Adorned in ragged poetry and songs,
I write and sing to rid the world of wrongs.

Guitar Breeze

A lonely guitar breeze
        strums
the memories of his mind

and everywhere he looks
        he finds

                short flashes of white,
                a fading twilight;

                        but no respite,
                        no saving grace
                        to light the night.

        He's an outlaw riding
    with an old dusty heartache
                and
            the dull fading glint
        of an old rusty keepsake.

                    There's emptiness
                    all around
                in the cradle of night.

            And
    with the dying of the light
                a lonely guitar breeze
                is stirring old memories

                        ,,, some better left
                        unawakened.

A Statue

An old guitar
with broken strings.

Music
with no score.

I stand
inside my loneliness,

a statue,
nothing more.

Dried Flowers Of Youth
for Rex Howard, July 23, 1930 - November 7, 2012
British Columbia Country Music Hall of Fame inductee 2004

Dried flowers of youth crushed between pages.
Forgotten utterings of ancient sages.
A whisper and scream and the drama between.
Life unravelling at the seam.
A young man running through early chapters.
Hobbling toward final ever afters.

You leave this world more every day.
Slowly you're slipping and sliding away
into that nether land of yesterday.
And oh, that I could follow you there:
To leave behind this worry and care.
To build with you castles on the beach
in that world you visit when you're out of reach.

Whispers and memories of your sweet song.
When you were young. When you were strong.
Before the years made your bones ache.
Before your hands started to shake.
Before you had to be wheeled in a chair.
Before time left you nothing to spare.

Dried flowers of youth are crumbling now
gracing the stage in their final bow.
Your frailty of heart will soon set you free
and far, far you'll fly away from me
to a place where streets are paved with gold.
Where dreams cannot be bought or sold.
Where music never ceases to play.
It will call to you softly and take you away.

And as you leave this world behind ...
the best part of me will become undefined.

Dancing To A Memory

Still, I hear that distant sweet song.
It whispers to me as I walk along
recalling those old familiar places
where love put us gently through her paces.

Although you're gone, sometimes you seem near.
I feel your touch but I know you're not here.
Each day I leave this world a bit more
as I inch ever-closer to death's door.

Dancing to a memory long since gone,
like a haunting song you linger on.
But somehow I've forgotten the words.
They've flown away on the wings of lost birds.

And if I chance to stand in God's grace
I fancy, again, I'll see your face.
Then each lonely year and tear will fade
as I lay down to rest in your warm shade.

> *And later*
> *in a distant dream*

Dancing to a memory long since gone
I still hear that sweet familiar song.
Then suddenly I'm standing in God's grace.
I hear your voice and then I see your face.

You are the music and I am the score
as we sway together inside heaven's door.

Dead And Gone

The days of yesterday are dead and gone.
But are they really? Or do some live on?
All time is happening now the scientists say,
so can we influence our yesterday?

If this idea proves to be the case
there's so many sorrows I'd erase.
I'd show my parents just how much I care.
And those unspoken loving thoughts I would share.

I'd rescind every tear I caused to fall.
Each angry word uttered I would re-call.
There are so many wrongs that I'd correct.
I'd treat all my loved ones with true respect.

When we're young we're folly to the truth.
I saw only myself inside my youth.
Time and tide relentlessly move on
and now the chance to make things right seems gone.

But somewhere in the universe's song
I think there's lyrics to right every wrong.
I'll find a way to recompose the score
as I re-enter life's revolving door.

They say our yesterdays are dead and gone,
but are they really? Or do they live on?

One Chord

We are one chord of rhythm and spirit
inside love's symphony.

A quiet quest of music
winding toward Nirvana's tone
as we strive to arrive
at the celebration of our being
and the joining of our souls;
and the repletion,
the second coming of completion.
A complexity made simple.

In the disarray of stars
you are the sun and I am the moon.
Then you are the moon and I am the sun
                    revolving,
                              evolving
                    we're coming undone
          in the spin of divine attrition
shadow dancers completing our mission.

I am you and you are me
We are one chord
of rhythm and spirit
becoming each other
inside God's symphony of soul.

One Heartbeat Away

I'm dry inside this falling rain.
Time and 15 streets away,
these age old streets connect again
in shimmering, long-ago display.

I spy a lovely butterfly
with glistening wings, passing by;
and oh that I could fly to you
and turn our yesterdays anew.

I close my eyes and move through time;
through music, rhyme and pantomime.
I see you standing in the light
glowing in the dark of night.

You're only one heartbeat away.
I want to come, but I must stay.
I hear the sound of Earthly things:
Children's laughter. Playground swings.

And so reality steps in.
I'm back inside time's Siamese twin.
You're only one heartbeat away.
I long to come, but I must stay.

One kiss and one embrace away.
I long to come ... but I must stay.

Atmosphere And Rhythm

The stage is empty,
waiting for the musicians and instruments.
Waiting for the players and singers
to give it melody, voice and mood.

The room is filling up
with audience and drinkers
waiting for the band to start
to give rhythm to the atmosphere.

The room starts swaying
to the inimitable beat.
The sitters stand to become dancers
to swing to the mood of the song.
The floor starts vibrating
        to the rising body heat.

            Audio radiance
        for the radiant audience.

Then four hours later the stage is empty.
        The room is empty
                but the ebbing atmosphere
        still holds hands with the fading rhythm.

The room closes its eyes,
                rejuvenates the atmosphere,
        revives the rhythm
    and re-imagines the dancers ...
            still dancing.

            And ...
            the beat goes on.

Musical Magic

You come to me softly in dreams at night
beckoning me through the hazy twilight
at the edge of a broken dissolving dawn
where everything but the dream is gone.

The orchestra's tuned for a rock symphony.
I'm writing this song to you from me.
And all my days bittersweet and tragic
are blown away in this musical magic.

I'm chasing my shadow outrunning the sun,
Llacing it up as it comes undone.
There's a taste to the air not there before
leaving me hungrier and wanting more.

And all my days bittersweet and tragic
are blown away in this musical magic.

This beautiful musical magic.

The Birds Of Prey

A Nightingale's copper voice sang in the trees
serenading angels gliding on the breeze.
A lonely Robin's song announced the end of fall.
Winter heard its voice and came running to its call.

Under the haloed sky of a fresh winter dawn,
in a forest glade I saw a mother and fawn.
And carved into a cedar tree, a woodpecker's profile;
a beautiful acrylic painting in a surreal style.

Then I saw the birds of prey fly wingless overhead
chanting in soft choruses to the newly dead.
And I was wont to say the measure of things I heard
that caused the crows to caw.at the mockingbird.

A nightingale's copper voice cried through the sky.
The birds of prey were sad but could not cry.

They flew tearless through the night,
hearts engorged with pity.
They flew wingless lost in time
above the winter city.

Burnt Out Torch Song

The glittering eye of the crow
and the weary eye in the sky
bead down on a pale forest glade
of watery reflections,
measuring the haphazard drift of the lily pads
in relation to the velocity of the breeze.

A haunting melody,
drifts through the trees at the shoreline;
a burnt-out torch song plays
for the grim reaper of love,
the dream keeper of heartaches.
Broken dreams, and tarnished memories
reflecting in the eye of the crow
      linger in the mist
        in the midst
of these matchstick-men trees.

A hazy shadow, a ghost crow
pirouettes to the sky symphony.
rising in a slow swirl of mist.
His eyes grow wet. He sheds a tear.
It lays gently on a dampened lily pad
then slips noiselessly
into the watery reflections,
echoing in the deafness like silent thunder,
striking the matchstick-men in the heart.

The burnt-out torch song flickers, then dies
     as the eye of the crow closes
   and the lid of the sky slams shut.

     The haunting melody
       lingers
    in the sticky fingers
  of the dark honeyed night
     closing in.

Catchers In The Rye

In a cavalcade of an electric sound-scena
the thundering drums cracked the ice of the arena
and caught the skaters blades in the cracks
which made the pros look like amateur hacks.

But the people weren't there to see the skaters.
They came to hear E.L.O.s showdown daters.
The ice turned into a springboard dance floor
and the crowd and dancers cried out for more.

Jeff Lynne stood on Jacob's ladder's top rung.
Request upon request was taken and sung
E.L.O. stacked the sound loud and sky high
pitching their songs to the catchers in the rye.

The sweet tough and mellow Lynne guitar riffs
woke up the dead and the freshly slabbed stiffs.
Everyone swayed back and forth with the beat
that was groovin' down tough and comin' up sweet.

Later swingin' loose on the moon and the stars
and the smackin' beat of the rockin' guitars.
the audience floated home on a sky high
knowing the were the catchers in the rye.

Deep Silver Silence Of Song

The darkness bites and cracks the snow and ice
   to wrinkle and slice the silence.
When the light falls on winter evenings
and the river makes no sound in its passing,
I watch and listen in reverence and awe.
   Its reeds, frozen stiffer than glass,
    are mute in this cold, cold silence ...
a silence that cannot be described or traversed.

At a moment like this, bathed in indigo and white,
   how can one anticipate the dawn?

But it does come, anticipated or not,
and slowly climbs over the tree-lined horizon.
   A blaze of sunlight
thawing the frost-bitten land sea and sky
into an evanescent kodak memory
of July daze and August haze.
A promise to glaze the beach and shore
   with fresh sand and rain
for the coming of feather, shell, mica and quartz
as the higher ground cedars and shale
whisper to the wind of days and nights to come

   At a moment like this
bathed in gold and turquoise,
   how can one not recall
hot, scorching summer evenings too?

   Then as quickly as it manifested
   the ice cracks, the bite goes slack
    and the darkness abates.

   Nature thunders in
and the anticipated thaw emerges
in a deep silver silence of song.

Heartbeat Of Existence

In the tangible realm of reality
its my soul that deftly composes
the religion of my rhythm,
in the den of tranquil reveries,
allowing me to walk on air
in a sea of melodic verse
reeling, rocking and rolling
in the heartbeat of existence.

>   Gulls soar and dip
>   on the river's wet lip
>   as chickadees whistle
>   inside bush and thistle;
>   and the ravens fly high
>   in a bright sunlit sky
>   with precision and persistence
>   in the heartbeat of existence.

Dawn and dusk, sisters in silence,
in the magic of constellations,
hold hands with time and tide
as I sway in sacred dance
and musical composition
in the pulse of consolation
and the heartbeat of existence.

Laying Soft Upon My Heart

A glimpse of steel, a flash of train
silent on the endless track,
and oh that I could ride again
the rails and not look back.

You still waltz across my mind,
a tender wistful melody,
and in those moments lost I find
the music brings you back to me.

We travelled light with heavy hearts
and rusty throats that could not sing:
Victims of our own false starts.
Dragging winter into spring.

I hold a ticket in my hand.
The destination is unknown.
I've crossed the line drawn in the sand
and common sense has long since flown.

But still you waltz across my mind,
a mellow Monet work of art;
and in those moments lost I find
you laying soft upon my heart.

A mellow Monet work of art ...
laying soft upon my heart.

The Rhythm Of Romance

One day I set my lonely feet
to dancing down a lonely street.
A place where I once chanced to meet
two other kindred dancing feet.

Our feet stood in a different stance
but kept the rhythm of the dance.
I felt the music fill my soul;
a symphony of rock'n'roll.

We talked of many splendid things:
of diamond rings and rainbow strings,
the joys a daydream often brings,
and my heart felt like it had wings.

And now my aching weary feet
have lost the address of that street
where timeless time and tide criss-cross.
And I am poorer for the loss.

I'll find my good foot once again
and come in from this freezing rain
that's left a blurry wet ink stain
reverberating in my brain.

I'll search until I chance to meet
those same two long lost dancing feet
that I once met within the sweet
of savored memories on life's street.

We'll hear the music's soft refrain.
We'll answer to its call again
and we will dance a sweeter dance
inside the rhythm of romance.

Rounders

You met me in a seedy bar at my very worst.
You were drinking vodka shots
　　　　　trying to quench a thirst.
I was packing six-guns looking for a kill.
You were waiting to be subjugated to my will.

The wind was like a saxophone playing through a flute
trying to encircle the square of its square root.
I was waiting for the symphony to start
to take another broken piece from my aching heart.

Then the music started and the heavens opened up
filling me with whiskey dreams that overflowed my cup;
but whiskey dreams are fleeting
　　　　　not meant to stay the course
so I strapped my gun belt on and saddled up my horse.

You were just a lonesome cowboy
　　　　　　tryin' to quench his thirst.
I was comin' off a heartache and at my very worst.

And now as I look back
　　　　on the dance floor's tilted track
we didn't have a chance ...
　　　　　should have said no to the dance.

We stumbled on love's dance floor
　　　　　　and a hungry thirst
Yeah, both of us were rounders ...
　　　　　together we were cursed.

The Sparkle Of A Distant Star

Under the sparkle of a distant star,
a piano solos in soft blue notes
writing scripture on the air.
I walk along a pier of dreams
above the waters of an ebb tide.
beneath a blur of pale bruised sky.

Reflections
ebb and flow
reverberating down a rabbit hole
        into the nothingness
        that leads to everything
where I am part of the drifting haze.

The silence is never-ending and thick
yet, somehow, I still hear your voice,
        vibrating on a violin string,
        slowly becoming a chord,
                a melody,
        a song in the emptiness
                leading to everything.

I will follow the sounds
of the violin and piano
                to the sparkle of that distant star
                        that leads to everything ...
                that leads to where you are.

The Days Of Old Gold

I carry old, tattered photos with me
from yesterdays etched in my memory.
There's a picture of us in a blue cabaret
where our favorite weekend band used to play.

I carry lost days in the back of my mind
and I never know when they'll start to unwind.
The old days are with me wherever I go.
You're still in my soul. I want you to know.

The days of old gold have come and gone.
They've faded away like yesterday's song.
Winter's arrived with gray clouds and rain
and the days of old gold won't come again...

No, the days of old gold won't come again
but deep in my soul you'll always remain.

The Strum

A silver guitar gleams in the moonlight
pressed to the lips of a star shining bright.
There's a mystic shroud draped over the night
and a song being born just out of sight.

The clock is ticking. It's half-past eleven
and I'm dreaming of you this side of heaven.
I patiently wait for the door to swing wide.
Two steps forward, one back, then inside.

The silver guitar has beckoned me here
from behind the veiled drape opaque and sheer.
The band is playing a sweet melody;
our favorite song for just you and me.

So I side-step the storm and walk into the light
and the glow of angels just out of sight.
The music always brings me to you
on the soft underbelly of roses and dew.

Then every gray sky turns to baby blue
as I lie in the strum of me and you.

To Visualize The Dream

Music invents the invisible to visualize the dream.
A conscious unconscious square root of the stream.

The rhapsody that flows into the eager heart
has no middle, no end and doesn't have a start.
It's always been incendiary lying deep beneath,
the beneficial residue of heaven's bequeath.

Music plays with secrets in the pale surreal.
Lyrics and harmonics blend to make us feel
the sought after emotions of love's contentment.
Each note, chord and passage are all heaven sent.

Music invents the means to visualize the dream:
The subconscious indivisible unraveling at the seam.

Water And Rain

I long to go down to the shore again:
To hear the water sing to the rain.
To see the seagulls fly on high.,
To hear the sadness in their cry.

The tender years when I was young,
when rainbows 'round my shoulders hung.
Those sky-blue days of golden tears.
These sky-blue eyes long for those years.

The long and winding path grows pale.
The mast now hung with ragged sail
sits alone on a desolate shore
and I'll hear the seagulls nevermore.

Youth's fleeting magic is long gone.
Life's music now a fading song.
The sky-blue skies have turned to gray
and soon my soul will fly away.

The days of life are beginning to fade,
an age-old stain on invisible suede.
And I long to go down to the shore again
to hear the water sing to the rain ...

to hear the water sing to the rain.

We'll Fly No More

We walk amongst the feathered strings
    we fashioned from our broken wings.

        We'll fly no more
        to songs of old.
            We'll dance no more.
            Our love's grown cold.

Robbed of our songs and sighs
    we disappear from each other's eyes
    down a highway of wounds and scars
    beneath a sky of burnt out stars.

We're flightless earthbound birds:
    With no music.
    With no score.

        We've come undone.
        We'll fly no more.

Hardened

If these trees hardened,
  then splintered,
  they'd make the ear-splitting music
    of ice-cold screams;
  and the grass would shriek
    in a chorus
  of a thousand deaths,
  reminiscent of the day
your heart hardened
  and mine splintered
    and our souls split
  into the cold death
    of the broken music
  we'd never, ever play again.

Heartache's Aftermath

In the blue purple sheen of a new midnight sky
a soft song lingers and then waltzes by.

The dance floor's emboldened with shades of blue light
alive with gold footprints on heaven's path;
but there are no dancers
                    where there should be dancers
and I'm lost in the blur of heartache's aftermath.

The air coiled 'round my voice curls and lingers
and winds tightly through my cold stiffened fingers.
I can't write my message or show my intention
and the ice in my heart is beyond comprehension.

There are no eyes present to look into my eyes.
In this blue purple sheen my world's in disguise.
I'm alone on this dance floor adrift on a dream
and the gold footprints never were
                    what they would seem.

I'm sailing on hope and a boat I can't steer
and the dance floor and dancers have all disappeared,
I'm alone searching for my lost other half
in the bruised atmosphere of heartache's aftermath,

In the blue purple sheen of a new midnight sky
        a soft song lingers
                and then ...
                    waltzes by.

The Amber Glow

The pale fading sky
longs for old violin strings
and the brush of a dusty bow
to compose a melody
that burns a bluer shade of amber
in the burnished orange embers
that still flicker in the ether.

This visual, staining my soul,
vibrates with a stir of echoes
that travel the canyons of my mind
in search of old strings
to hang a song high.

High enough
to serenade the stars
and shine the amber glow
a bluer shade of gold.

Leading Me Home

The silence of the roses
    is kin to the rain.
The kiss in your eyes
    is kin to my heart.

I climb through the magic of unborn hours
    into the mystery of your voice
        alive with the songs I used to sing.

There is a bird in the room that only I can see
    but somehow you have managed to hear
        the flutter of its feathers,

    The rhythm of its wings
        marries your melody
           to my lyrics
    and a song is born from us
        for us.

    The silence of the roses
        and the kiss in your eyes
        are leading me
           to the song we are.

Leaving The Harbor

Enjoying
the calm of the harbor
the sailboats lazily roam
the tranquil shorelines.

Navigating
the gentle twists and turns
of the Nicomekl River
they move to the beat
of old saltwater dreams.

Heading
toward the call of the ocean
and the keening of gulls
the sailboats waltz in tandem,
leaving the harbor.

Looking, Not Seeing

I stand at the cracked escarpment
  of your weather-beaten heart
  whispering sugar-sweet rumors
    of lost love recovered
     from the depths of oblivion.

I stand beneath a million stars
  screaming silent songs
    to the melodies your heart is playing.

My songs ebb and flow
  wordlessly
    past you:
  imagined symphonies for the deaf,
  silent ballets performed for the blind.

And all the while,
  you look through me
    and past me.

  But you never see me ...
    you never see me.

Periwinkle Pond

The periwinkle pond sparkles
at the edge of the gathering flowers.

> In the dark of the wood,
> deep within the trees,
> a song is being born.

A technicolour painting
splashed onto nature's canvas
begins to sway in the breeze.

> A melancholy blue note
> skates across the still of the pond
> toward the distant city shore,
> tuning the strings of streetlamp glow
> to the music of approaching stars.

As twilight dims the face of day,
the periwinkle pond enters night's dream
> then slowly falls asleep
> inside the sky's lullaby.

Phantom Moon

Ekphrastic poem by Candice James written to the painting "Phantom Moon" by Hermine Weiss and Candice James

Midnight blue and twilight mauve
gather the night into a lullaby
above a sparkling turquoise stream;
and all the while
the phantom moon shimmers.

A gang of audience trees whispers
swaying in the audio radiance
of slick ravens crying soft overhead;
and all the while
the phantom moon glistens.

A haunting ambiance
spills onto this moment of grace
for a moment,
for all time,
for almost no time at all;
and all the while
the phantom moon listens ...

rapt in the spin
of a star passing by
the phantom moon stands watch.

The Crows And I

Beneath a darkening sky
    I hunker down on a solid branch
        in dark sacrosanct prayer
      with the crows of midnight's passage
    waiting for the shimmering needle of moonlight
      to sew our thoughts together.

The fluttering of prayer rises in my throat
    and comes to rest on ebony wings
      and a deep knowing the crows understand
    resonates in the echoes of this surreal forest.

The wind rustles the branches
    like metal brushes on a snare drum;
      an orchestra section of leaves comes alive
    in a woodwind symphony of sound,

    Its staccato and legato etch messages
      onto the black sable coat of night
        chaining her kiss to the wind
      wounding the sky with the cut of her lips
      as strange songs seep
          from the needle of moonlight
      dripping indecipherable lyrics
    that only the crows and I understand.

The Dance

Shall we dance?
>I ask the shadows
>>that haze through my hazy days
>>>and haunt my dreams at night.

>I whisper to the wind
>>and speak to the stars
>>>and then ...
>>>>the music starts.

I stand at the sidelines,
>back to the wall,
>>waiting for a chance to dance ...
>a lonely wallflower
>>on time's timeless stage.

>I am a shadow,
>>a fading ink stain
>>>on a dog-eared page of life.

>>>Losing my balance
>>and losing my breath
>I haze and blend into the shadows
>and become the dream
>>I am dreaming.

I let go of the last thread of life
>>as it breaks ...
>then the music stops
>>and the dance begins.

The Song I Am

The heart that stains the rose with blood
cries to the wind for a softer song
as it dances on glass in steel heeled stilettoes.

Paper maché and origami notes
spar for position on the freshly bled thorns
of teardrops and sighs echoing the sweet
in this symphony penned for the weak and the frail.

And, somewhere in this ice-cold world
a prisoner of love is writing my name
on a tombstone meant for somebody else.

In a film clip I've suddenly become privy to
there's a whiskey filled memory and a blood-stained rose
holding my heart to account for a lie
as the crystal hands of time
shatter the dance floor of glass I stand on
and squeeze the song I am to death
crushing my bittersweet tears to the bone...
      and then ...
           the music stops.

Voices Of Yesterday

Today,
      pale music from the past
            fills every room in my mind.
                  A thousand indigo veins
            paint the cracks in my aching heart.

Voices from yesterday
      approach from all directions.
            The fading blue from my eyes
      runs like watercolor down my cheeks.

In the mirror, I'm fading to grey, to pale, to invisible.
      The full moon has fallen to its knees
            and broken the fragile string of life.

Today,
      I am sinking into deep water
            the color of pastel music:
                  a sweet serenade
            sung by the voices of yesterday ...
                  the voices I know so well.

White Swans At Midnight

The white swans at midnight
shone stark in the moonlight
as we strolled holding hands
on the white silver sands.

Near those glistening birds
in the womb of our words
our hearts opened up
as we sipped from love's cup.

The world was a song
as we walked along
two stepping through time
in our own private rhyme.

Then the world shifted
and our hearts drifted.
I remember that day
when you walked away.

The white silver sands
had slipped through our hands
and the white swans at dawn
disappeared with our song.

Home At Last

There is a scattering of strange magic
    hidden beneath the stones of fantasy
        I so easily step up to and dance on.

From the depth of a dream
    music begins to surface
        on a pond of still water.

    With the vibrations
        from my mind
    I write the lyrics of myself
        and the melody of you
    onto the waters of eternity
that I may slip into your song
        and find myself.

        I spin effortlessly,
    inside the sway of a song
too beautiful to be heard,
        home at last.
          At peace.

Breath And Song

I breathe in the air
    and create the atmosphere.
I breathe in the emotion
    and create the ambiance.

I exhale
    and the mood evolves.

I breathe in the words
    and create the lyrics.
I breathe in the music
    and create the melody.

I exhale
    and the song is born.

        Breathe in.
        Breathe out.

        Inhale.
        Exhale.

In your own unique rhythm
    become your own song.

Heartbeat Of The Stars

Sorrow rides me like the crave rides an addict.
If I close my eyes, I forget who I am for a moment.

I reach for loud music and noise.
It fills my mind up
to the brim of its Stetson edge
until I'm not aware of myself anymore.
I ride the smoke of a wish
and cast my sorrow to an unkind wind
riddled with cruel intentions.

I walk through the distant stars
and listen to aliens reciting poems
and musicians searching through symphonies
for the lost chords of their youth.

In the core of a beautiful love song,
and the poetry of my greatest sorrows,
I listen to the heartbeat of the stars
and am comforted by the realization
... this too shall pass.

If I open my eyes, I'll disappear forever
into the song I am ...
                              so,
                    I slowly open my eyes.

I Sang You A Love Song

I wrote you a love song
    with my bones and blood.

    It sounded like breath forming
      and angels kneeling.

I sang you the love song I wrote.

    My bones splintered
      and my blood spilled
    as you flowed
      into my soul.

Inside The Forest Of Song

I am the old seed of music
        vibrating in the forest of song
                echoing in the clef of the moon
                        and the score of the sun.

I speak to the universe
        through the dampened lips
                of a runaway dream.

        I am
                the ragged notes of hope
        resting in the sacred sounds of eternity
                whispering
        inside the forest of song.

        I am the old seed of music
                waiting to be reborn
                        again and again.

Piano Of Secrets

A fabulous melody
        is playing in my mind.
                So familiar ...
                        but I can't quite grasp it.
                It's too far away to recognize.

And there's a piano of secrets
            chording my heart
with black and white fingers.
                    Beckoning me to find it's name.
                    Hiding in the shadows of my soul.

I'm gazing into a waxed ebony mirror
            trying to find an ember of myself,
                    still aglow,
                            in this sea of emptiness
                                I swim in all alone.

I am the shadow shape
                of a song nobody knows.
        I am a friend to musical instruments.

I am consort to the piano of secrets
            that plays me as I am;
                    not as the world sees me.

Play The Rose For Me
(Ekphrastic poem to painting by Lavana La Brey)

She rises above the music
in keys and ethereal tones,
drifting through Nirvana nights
and metaphysical zones.

Dressed in velvet and lace
and shades of gray, black and white,
the piano keys become stepping stones
leading her into the light.

Old melodies cascade and flow
on a rolling tapestry of thought
and what this lady most would seem
that she most is not.

Wishing on a midnight star
she states her wistful plea:
Wrapped in a long ago memory
she whispers, "Play *'The Rose'* for me."

The Violin

The violin's waxed mahogany face,
　　　the silk of the strings,
　　　　　and the glide of the bow
　　　　　　　coax the music out
　　　from under the maestro's touch.

　　　　　Illusion and reality blend
　　　　　in sweet magnificence.

　　　　　Surreal and concrete sounds
　　　　　　flow effortlessly
　　　　　　　in a magical weave.

There is a majesty to this music
　　　　　played by the ghosts of my past
　　　　　　reflecting within
　　　　　the violin's waxed mahogany face.

Thin Sleep

The songs have forgotten their names.
The music has forgotten its score
and the sounds of silence are there,
and then suddenly ...
        they're not there.

Memories have been lost at sea
and heartaches have piled up
on a lonely beach of shipwrecked dreams;
as unrecognizable as pebbles
        turned to sand.

Everything sleeps a thin sleep here.
Restless. Half here; half there.
Somewhere, inside this fog I've become,
the songs have found their names
scrolled up in the scrawl of the night;
and the music has found its runaway notes
too luscious and thick to remain
in the clutch of a wandering silence.

        The song wants to row a boat.
        The music wants to ride a train

        This push and shove will pass.

The words
perched on the piano keys
will remember their timing and place.

The tones,
sleeping inside the ivories and ebonies,
will awaken with an eloquent ease
and climb slowly to a coveted crescendo
then fall softly back into that moment
of infinite forgetfulness:
where it all began,
where it all ended.

I lie on a beach of shipwrecked dreams.

A seagull flies overhead
crying for what did not come to pass.

The words and the music,
are married forever and ever
and they keep playing
      over and over again.

        Over and over again
        inside this thin sleep
        of the all.

We Danced

We danced for a while.
to simple music.

Later when I tried to sleep he was coiled,
cold and shivering against my chest.
I felt the better part of him slipping away
into the other room of another night.

I heard him sobbing.
I listened to him cry
even though I knew I shouldn't have.
His sorrows were so massive.
His tears fell wet on my heart.

He slipped back into my bed
and coiled into my soul.
He pressed his cheek to mine
and wiped away the tears
that bled from my heart,
in tribute to his sorrows.

We danced for a while to simple music
and then one night he slipped away
into that other room,
that other night forever
and the music simply died.

Birds On A Wire (sonnet)

You touch my soul like blazing prairie fire;
like morning dew on windblown desert rose.
Our wings electric; fire birds on a wire,
tips rapt in passion as it sparks and glows.
The wire song pierces deep into our hearts
with mystic rhythms softly tunneling.
Inside these sacred canyons music starts
with notes from horns of plenty funneling
into a rhapsody of precious song.
Safe, locked inside each other's warm embrace,
as soft as feathers yet steel tensile strong,
we trace the love lines on each other's face.

Birds on a wire with burnt electric wings.
Electrocution savoured as love sings.

A Statue

An old guitar
with broken strings.

Music
with no score.

I stand
inside my loneliness.

A statue ...
nothing more.

Defining Moment

There is always
a certain defining moment:

> In each poem.
> In each painting.

In each musical composition
> and in each life.

> You are my moment
> and my definition.

Deep Gold Frost And Soft Silver Songs

Plunged into the depth of forever
we swam through a deep gold frost
            to the other side of the stars.

There were violets and lilacs,
            and soft silver songs
                  drifting through symphonies;
                        a dream within a dream.

                  I was living inside your eyes
            for the fifty-first thousandth time,
                  still amazed
            at the newness of the atmosphere
                  and cherishing every breath.

Unravelling on a fast-spinning spool,
            I became a wire afire,
                  alive in a quicksilver flame.

There were palominos and stallions
            dancing at the edge of my heart
            and I was revolving, evolving,
                  dissolving ...
            inside each echo and beat.

In the flaming rings of a Pegasus yoke
            I saw the true darkness
                  riding behind your eyes:
                        torn and tossed,
                  adrift and lost
            on an ocean of deep gold frost.

As I watched you turn to ice,
            the soft silver songs turned to stone.

100

Dance With The Surprises

Taste the mist of a shooting star.
Ride the surf of the Milky-Way,
Climb to the edge of a shimmering moonbeam
and slide down its highway of dreams.
    Embrace the moment
    and dance with the surprises.

Stop at the door with double locks.
Find the keys within yourself.
Stand at the edge of uncertainty
and dive into the river of chance.
    Embrace the moment
    and dance with the surprises.

Listen to the whispering wind.
Walk through the echoes of the rain.
Swim in the sea of a pristine snowflake
and rest in the arc of a pastel rainbow.
    Embrace the moment
    and dance with the surprises.

Open up your heart and soul.
Keep your spirit flowing free.
Hear the rhythm of the universe.

And when the music plays,
    dance ...

Dance with the surprises.

Dancing In The Dark Alone

Drifting on invisible waves, almost asleep,
hazy voices at the edge of my hearing, beckon me.
      I rise in wisps of white smoke
         into the ebony night sky
          travelling toward you.

        Stopping mid air.

         I Hover lazily,
uncertain, anxious, edgy,
until I see the white smoky
outline of your figure
approaching me knowingly.

Closer, closer;
      I feel your breath on mine.
The atmosphere becomes electric
      as we spin together.

      Dancing in the dark, to the end of love,
we are the unfinished symphony
rising in surreal white smoke rings,
lost in the shadows of time.

      Dancing in the dark alone,
        I always dance with you.

Eulogenic – *(In Memory Of Rex Howard)*
Inducted into BC Country Music Hall of Fame 2004
(July 23, 1930- November 7, 2012)

A frozen tear on my cheek
mirroring my heart.
A cold wind, a hard rain.
Winter's settling in.

Sweet gentle soul of my heart
you were too beautiful for this world;
too beautiful for me
and yet you loved me
through it all.

I search the empty spaces
for a glimpse of you:
A touch. A fragrance.
A knowledge that you're near.

It's too great a sorrow
to think you're gone,
truly gone.

Some things never come again.
And some forever remain.

You're gone
and this frost on my heart
holds no promise
of a silver thaw.

The music has faded.
The curtain has fallen.

The stage is set in stone.

A frozen tear on my cheek.
A cold frost on my soul.

Flamenco Fire Dance

Inside the of the eye of the cat
twilight explodes through a blazing yellow iris,
teeming with colours, tones, and surreal figures.
And then the dance begins.

The kaleidoscope swirl of flame and dress,
the smacking click of boots on floor,
      the whirl of wind,
        the twirl of time
rolling in on staccato waves.

A tsunami of sound,
rhythm pounding the ground.
Hollowed out bones
beating torrid moments
to a sweet sacrificial death
inside the hot hurried breath
of desire on a wire,
stepping into the fire
of the dance.

Dimensionalization of the flesh.
Spirit sparks and liquid lightning.
Icy-hot, fiery-cold.
Bottled and sold
on the dance floor of dreams,
in the house of yellow lights,
in the eye of the cat,
and the double distilled
    single malt heat
       of the
   flamenco fire dance.

Fluid Silence

There is a fluidity to this silence.
    A timeless tango
dancing to the whisper of a familiar song:
    The strong, silent type.
    Tall, dark and handsome.

There is a flexibility to this fluidity.
Slow to rapid,
vapid to deafening.
Spinning
within its own harness,
dangling
on a string,
thinning to thread,
quickening to rope.

Encircling my thoughts in its net.

    Becoming sound.
    Becoming music.

      The same familiar song.
      The same timeless face.

    You always waltz
    in perfect rhythm
    through the fluid silence
    of my every reverie.

Guitar Strings

The guitar strings shimmer in the light.
A starburst haloes the room
spinning the dust in my mind,
spoking through the wheels of time;
and I see a ring of flaming water and stars
burning the edge off the night.

I move closer into the heat of the moment.
I swim through the midnight stars
into a raw red rhapsody
in the shimmering ring
of bright water and slick wet whispers
to dance in the dark of your heart
once again...

and then ...

the guitar strings
slowly fade to silence;
and the music stops
as the ceiling flies away
and the room disappears.

Justin Bieber And The Blue Petal Dream

Peeking through the blue petal dream
Justin shows his split personality
with one vacant eye, the left one
and one frantically focused eye, the right one,
although it could be the erroneous one
which would then make the left one... the right one.
Justin likes to think about these puzzles
when he is hiding safely
inside his carefully crafted disguise
at the crinkled center corner
of the blue petal dream he's constructed.

Sable brushes dip and ooze colors
onto the spinning grooved canvas drape.
There are small creature masks
and burnt out Olympic torches
adorning the face of the rippled vase
and there are breezes blowing inside the bouquet
tousling Justin's hair every which way,
loosening the pins of propriety
making him giddy with anticipation.
He heard the gossip of the leaves
Rustling with news of a water change.

The water change is always the highlight of the week
for Justin and the blue petal dream.
When the gurgle and beat of the water begins
Justin fantasizes a torrid tango.
The blue petal dream fantasizes a Blue Danube waltz,
and the chaotic dance that ensues
between these two unlikely partners
is a sight to behold; a revelation; an apocalypse now.

As the band rocks on in red hot chords,
peeking through this blue petal dream
we see the real Justin Bieber...
the one who can't dance.

Night Shift

The night shifted
into a purple movement
of dance and desire.
under a fiery furnace of stars,
     We walked
through mists of dust and glory
holding hands and hearts
burning inside the glow of our passion.

     We waltzed
into the core of the music's ice blue fire,
waxing it hotter with our breath,
honing it to a wetter flame
by the depth of the kiss we carved
into the shifting night.

     We slid
through the purple movement
of dance and desire flawlessly,
and lay spent in the furnace of stars ...
embers sparking in the dust and glory,
waiting patiently inside the music
for the night to shift
once again.

No Trace

I took the little labels,
Identifying the frets,
off the Dobro last night.
Since we don't make beautiful music anymore,
I couldn't see much sense in keeping them on.
You wouldn't be trying to jam with me again
while I played the Fender guitar.

In a way it felt bad,
but in a way it felt so good
to peel those little labels off
just like you peeled my love off of you.

As I look at the Dobro now
there's no trace at all
that the labels were ever there.

If I chance to see you again
I'm just as certain
there'll be no trace on you
that I was ever there.

Opposite Deficiencies

At the crest of our opposite deficiencies,
we slid down a sloped oxymoron
punctuated by a dangling semi-colon.

We knew we had a list
of groceries for the soul
but we had misplaced it
somewhere along the way.

I thought of Nat King Cole
and wrote velvet and scotch
on the new list.

You mentioned James Brown
and wrote corduroy and rye
on the list.

Opposite deficiencies reared their ugly heads.
Too weary to dance or argue
we decide to sleep on it,
whatever "it" was.

Dawn broke a hot sun open.

In the light of day,
our opposite deficiencies
stared us down in glaring reality.

You danced out the door.
I hummed a King Cole tune;
grocery list not forgotten,
simply destroyed by an oxymoron
in the fallout of
our opposite wounded deficiencies.

In the end, it all comes down to
the music in our soul ...
                    the music we are.

110

Outside Heaven's Door

Weaving
through existential moments of hope
in the burnt-out dust of distant stars
and skating
on the thin cracking ice of creation's water

The weave and the water
lead me
to the edge of eternity

I stand
instrument and voice at the ready
pen and paper in hand
composing silent symphonies
outside heaven's door
waiting for God.

I Promise You This

I promise you this
even when we're miles apart,
hearts apart
and tears apart
I'll still be loving you.
I'll always be loving you.

You came into my life.
I became baptized.
I became new.
I became part of you.

Why are we so different?
We both eat, sleep, laugh, cry and dream
and yet we dance to different drummers.

You always say "I'm Leading"
but sometimes
your steps are too intricate for me to follow.

When the separation comes
as I know it must,
I promise you this.
We'll always dance in my dreams
even though the music's died.

I love you so much it hurts me.
Now, I realize, it always will.

Saturday Wishes

I'm Saturday wishes
from Friday's lips
      spent like a sailor
      on a Sunday hangover.

I'm slow moving syrup
and fast action dancing;
      a technicolour dream
      that lasts all night long.

I'm blues in the night,
love on the rocks
      and heart-wrenching ballads
      in minor seventh keys.

I'm the top of the mark,
the crème de la crème;
      I'm every song written
      rolled into one sound.

I'm Saturday wishes,
      stale on Sunday's breath,
            dancing another dream to death.

Sometimes I Dance

In the barren courtyard of my mind
        sometimes
                I dance
                        to remember.

                                Sometimes
                                I dance
                                to forget.

        Even when I dance alone
        I always dance with you.

There is a bittersweet haze
        wrapping its arms around me,
                whispering
        in a seductive, raspy voice.

        'You can stop dancing
            anytime you want
                but you can never leave.'

Day by day
        and night after night
                the dance lasts
                        longer and longer.

        Day turns into night.
        Night turns into day.

Through the haze
I hear my phone ringing.
                It just keeps on ringing
                        and ringing
                but I can't answer it ...
                I'm lost in the dance.

        Sometimes I dance to remember.
        Sometimes I dance to forget.

114

The Dance
(Sestina)

A wet moon hangs high in the sky
A shimmering snowball, a glistening eye
Tears spill out to star dust the night
Transparent against its ebony frame
A midnight sonata sets the mood
As angels dance on the winds of chance

Taking the risk factor out of chance
A pale crimson sunset blankets the sky
Blue notes echo an indigo mood
Invisible teardrops pool in the eye
Hidden behind the mind's ebony frame
The remnants of dreams lost in the night

A renegade twilight fled from the night
A doomed desperado without a chance
A delicate painting ripped from its frame
Stars wished upon fell from the sky
Dreams dissolved into lakes in the eye
Drowning torch songs dimming the mood

A soft tender kiss rekindled the mood
Taking the edge off the black brackish night
Uncovering secrets held in the sky's eye
Loading the dice hedging the chance
To catch a falling star from the sky
And set it aflame inside passion's frame

Now the mirror falls and shatters its frame
Knocking the dust off a neglected mood
A bright silver thread unzips the sky
A lost dream emerges from inside this night
With unrehearsed steps on the smooth winds of chance
To dance in the shadow of the moon's eye

Emotion spills from the pearl eye
Melting the ice off this ancient freeze frame

115

Begging me dance, take a risk, take a chance
Bending my heart and soul to its mood
A candle burning the dark off the night
The wet moon flickers high in the sky

I chance to dance through the needle's eye
I unzip the sky and polish its frame,
Changing the mood and colour of night.

The Depth Of The Dance

The fading sun on the sand dissolves
into moon drops on the water.
Waves sparkle and dance with diamonds
as old memories roll in.

I recall the young days of sunbeams and moonglow.
You and I casually playing with time and tide
as if they could never change,
as if we would never change.

When we walked our beach of dreams,
alive with the breath of angels,
we were sewn together in the womb of time:
A deep resonant symphony
vibrating inside the tidal music,
and we danced.
Oh how we danced.

Today, I walked that beach again,
alone, yet not alone.
I watched an amber sunset;
usher in an evanescent moon
over a surreal twilight ocean.

I stood, silently, on eternity's shore.
Haunting memories rolled in softly
on waves of enchantment
and danced with the pale ghosts of yesterday.
Oh how they danced.

Oh, how we danced!

I remember the depth of the dance.

117

The Dreamer Of Dreams

I

The moon rises
In the paling flare of a sultry day.
The sun disappears:
Fleeing marauding moonbeams;
As stars emerge in an ebony glazed sky.

A ghostly figure dances on the horizon.
The dreamer of dreams is weaving a dream
As gorgeous twilight waltzes in
Cloaked in lilac and indigo scarves
Stacked foot upon arm upon thigh upon chest.
We follow this pied piper, this dreamer of dreams
Through the thickening purple and indigo mist
Into the secret palace of mood music
and sparkling stars from whence he came.

An intangible aching claws its way out of the fold
And spills fire and rain in keys and tones
Onto the gleam of hollowed out bones,
Illuminating the hidden secrets twilight holds.

The eternal dreamer of dreams
Breathes on his fine sable brush
And paints us into his dream of liquid fire
And heavy water alive with songs.

II

Before we entered this dream:
we were empty songs filled with loneliness.
We were broken chords collapsed inside blurred music.
Our hearts were charred with the rain we burnt to ash.
So we shook the chill off the hard edge of night
and polished our charred hearts to coal; then to diamond
and yesterday's songs turned to dust and fell like rain
whetting our appetites for the depth of the dance.

In the crease and weave of the dream
baptized and reborn in sacred waters of the dance,
we polished the sky to glowing marble;
and composed new songs for the rain to sing;
and the dreamer of dreams
breathed a symphony onto his fine sable brush...
and painted a masterpiece.

The Pink Velvet Room

The rain drizzles down softly,
in a hazy opalescent mist, blurring my vision.
The street seems half remembered,
and yet somehow unfamiliar, until I reach the driveway
marked by the yellow broom tree and scarred white boulder.
I'm swept away on a magic carpet of haunting music.
Destination a ceramic, ivory door
with shiny, silver locks, glistening; basking lazily
in a lone golden sunbeam permeating the mist.

I stand anxiously at the door wondering how I'll enter,
then, out of the blue, an antique golden key
etched with my initials dances in the palm of my hand.
I open the door to one large room,
unsullied and untouched by time.
There is no past, no present, no future.
There is this music and this moment.
This ever-present, yet ever elusive now.

I step onto a sea of plush carpet and song
cresting and ebbing under my feet
inviting me into the dance of yesterday
as I wade deeper into this sea
of endless memories and eternal moments.
All fear vanishes as I enter into the soft afterglow
of this all-encompassing pink velvet room
alive with sunsets, moonbeams, stardust and dreams.

Glistening, in stature and opulence
beneath the rainbow streaked, crystal chandeliers,
two magnificent, mahogany, grand pianos
begin to play in perfect, continuous harmony.
I float toward them, on my own private cushion of air,
and run my eager hands, in a slow gentle motion,
over the pink satin piano seats,
feeling the vibrations flow through my fingers,
beating in unison with my heartbeats.
Haunting me; taunting me; bringing me fully alive.

I touch the cool ivory and ebony keys,
As melody, piano and mind become one,

Over in the corner, a hazy movement catches my eye.
Something ethereal tugs at my sleeve.
Suddenly, the pungent scent of Tabu perfume
invades this ghostly atmosphere;
The scent of a woman.
The scent of my mother.
The aroma and texture of childhood days.

Oh the carefree days of youth,
so far and yet, so near.
I swear I can almost taste their liquid essence
sliding down my throat, soothing, like milk and honey.

From childhood's page through middle age,
the smiles and tears, the hopes and fears
wrapped in piano strings and angel wings,
still breathe with a life of their own.

The music of my childhood.
The song I am.
The pink velvet room.
The lost dimension.
This is what dreams may come.

The Sands Of Eternity

Caught in the obtuse angle
Of a one-sided thought,
My mind circles
In square root patterns
On a dance floor of shifting sands.

Sparkles sewn
Into the pale gray dream I lay on
Form diagonal paths
Across the ink-stained pages
Of my consciousness.

In the distance,
Growing louder as it approaches,
A disembodied flute plays
In a harmony of circular echoes
Nuzzling the rain
Blowing kisses onto the wind.

I walk through sun shadows,
mind strum rainbow songs,
and sparkle for a brief moment in time.

Then, held in invisible dance,
I melt into the sands of eternity.

The Silence

I hear a fluttering of wings
in that still small silence
before the crow caws.

Like a small moth in my ear
something is calling to me.
An indistinct murmur at first,
beating louder
in unison with my heart.

I slide into myself,
a sleeping trombone
lying between tympani and trumpet,
amongst a muted gathering of instruments
anxious for release.

The wings flutter faster
in the still small silence
before the crow caws.

The crow spreads its wings,
bares its beak
and caws loudly.

Suddenly ...
the orchestra bursts into sound.

The silence shatters.

The Singer
(for Linda Jones)

She is:

        elegance,
        warm velvet,
           rainbow strings,
           music and song.

She moves,

        weaving in and out of his eyes,
           his heart, his soul.

Her voice

        awakens the white doves
           that lay sleeping
        in fields of lavender wishes.

She stands

        beneath a purple twilight sky.
           Stars begin to fall
            into her eyes.

She moves,

        weaving in and out of the music
           into his eyes.

She is:

        elegance, warm velvet,
          and rainbow strings.

            She is
          the music.

            She is
          the song.

Inside Out

I am lost
                In a bizarre wedding bell of sound:
                        Chaos marrying my evil twin
                        and I, the only uninvited guest

I mount a surreal cliff of clefs
                Latching onto a glory stone
                        .

I am safe
in the sweet sonorous pitch
                        And neon glow
                                of a moon-struck chord
                        Piercing the eye of midnight.

Rose petals and stardust whirl and swirl
                        of the opalescent dancers.
The pale ghosts of yesterday resurrected
And alive in the film clips and audio
Pulsating on the cutting room floor .
                        It's all so rhythmic
                                And...
                        So very, very cinematic

Decibel Rhythm

I'll never forget the decibel reading!

We joined in perfect silence;
a deafening amalgamation.

We were
elements of a separate merger
deliberately discharging each other
like a double barrelled shotgun.

      We were crafty:
      Side-stepping the toughs.
      Vetoing the bluffs.

We were volatile:
Gunpowder children.
Dancing the discos of thunder.
Ripping the dancefloors asunder.

I'll never forget the look on your face

as I two-stepped away in the tango of time
and waltzed away from your uneven rhythm.

Even now
          I remember the decibel reading
             and the look on your face.

      But I still can't remember
      the name of the song.

Disco Fever

Flashing, liquid lights.
Bouncing, beating music.
Masquerading rhythm.

Disco fever injects the atmosphere.

Feet come alive:
Jumping, shuffling, bumping, grinding.

Cushioned floors stretch like elastic:
Hammered, stomped, battered and bruised.

Disco fever infects the dancers:
A disease running rampant, coughing contagiously.
A virus run rampant, unvaccinated.

The walls resound and reverberate.
Pictures faint and fall.
Walnut panels ripple and waver
inside a jazzy dream.

The clock ticks terminally.
Disco fever infects hard hands.
Time runs out.

The music dies a quaffing death.
Plexus severed.

Disco fever mounts ...
then drowns in time.

Deciphering The Code

Black bonded paper
          and transparent ribbons
            are typing a note in the air.

It's almost like an invisible plane
        skywriting without any fuel.
          It's funny how you know it
        without reading or hearing.

It's strangely comparative
        to braille of the brain.
          Sensory receptors,
        tuned or untuned,
still pick up a sound wave of sorts.

It's all in the way you decipher the code.

        A rhapsody to one
        is acid rock to another.

Replacements

Finger-snapping brain waves
seem somehow out of tune these days.
Just like marabones and pickaninny gum;
especially if you still never got a black one
after spending five dollars in one shot.

Heavy acid rockers
       are lost on the waves of disco drum rolls;
             and some sneak has oiled
      each and every one of their fingers.
               They couldn't snap out of it
               even if they wanted to.

Hand-clapping nerve endings
are obliterating all the phalange fallacies
             we've been led to believe.

Looking through my binoculars
I see a semi-submerged hand in the ocean.

               I can barely hear the dull thud
                 of its futile fingers
              snapping and slapping;
                  thwapping and splashing.

                 Slowly fading away.

Music Spheres

She lies on a cushion of air.
    The music swirls around her
    like a Jacuzzi.

Jets of mystical steam
    escort her to a star
She floats on the Milky Way
    magic carpet ride.

The universe is midnight blue
    with black overtones.
The stars are like a traffic jam
     in a black-out:
      Cars turning and veering.
      Flickering signals.
      Disappearing headlights.

She threads her way through them
    like a supple needle.

Her electric-propelled carpet moves supersonically.
    Everything is unclear,
     unfocused,
    a split second blur.

She passes everything
    and sees nothing.

    She doesn't mind.
The music is all that matters.

Rippling

Rippling through a quantum leap
clouds become suns.
The moon turns inside out
and stars cry icicles
onto a neon glazed terrain.
A mountain erupts
in a river of rainbows
and arrows pierce the eye in the sky.

I stand on a shaky precipice,
perfectly balanced,
in time and in tune
with the chaotic flow.

Below me,
a fire pit blazing with spears.
Above me,
a lightning bolt humming a song.

I unstrap my dusty guitar from my back.
Pick in hand, I strum along
and the universe comes alive
with dance.

Rippling through a quantum leap ...
I become the song.

Fade Away

The days are broken chords.
The nights are alien music
sifting through the sands of time.

In the rivers of my dreams
your face swims toward me
in a pattern of hazy prisms.

You're alive somewhere
inflicting fresh wounds
on the snows of ages past.

I see your lips moving
but I can't hear you anymore.
You're too far away now.
Water penetrates your lungs.
You hover somewhere
in between the balance
of breath and suffocation.

I am not afraid
of your fading watery face,
and suddenly
I can feel myself becoming fascinated
by a strange new music surrounding me.

Fade away.
Fade away.

Face your own reality
and leave my dreams alone.

Coda

Then:

In a trilogy of tender torment
three words spilled from a satin shoe
and danced our dreams to death

I'm leaving you!

This orchestration of punctured sentiment
was out of tune
and we were out of time
in the legato
of a long overdue staccato
and suspended ending.

Now:

Sliding down a jagged treble clef
of silent screams
into the *'bass-ment'*
of booming reality,
our tangled tablature
weaves itself into a slick loose tempo
that can't be deciphered,
though the words ring out in striking clarity.

I'm leaving you!

In a singularity of certain death
and swift shot rebirth,
the trilogy of tender torment ends,
and a new song emerges...

Coda!

Mystic Moon

The staccato movements of a mystic moon,
hanging high and wet in the sky,
keep me tied to its secrets
as I dance in a solace of rings
creating a beautiful song.

Then suddenly,
an abrasive voice permeates the silence.
Space no longer sacred.
A child of a lesser God
has entered the realm of the mystic moon.

> *Out brief soiled spirit!*
> *This realm belongs to me.*
> *The fire in your eyes*
> *is burning the edge of this song,*
> *turning the music to ash.*

The legato movements of the mystic moon
whispered to me of the danger.
Warned me of your approach
before your abrasive essence
could destroy my song
and cremate my dream.

I trade secrets with the mystic moon
as we dance in a solace of rings
to compositions of the third kind
shining the music into a new song
casting a spell on the bars
solidifying the tempo and style
into an impenetrable wall of sound
that you may never enter.

Deep Blue Purple

I envision
>   a deep blue purple light,
>   perpendicular at first,
>   spreading into a horizontal dream
>   that I can lie in.

At the edges there are purple butterflies
>   and pale blue roses
framing the essence of the light.

>   I climb the white alabaster steps

>   Inside, the most beautiful music
>   permeates the atmosphere.

>   It creeps into my veins
>   and warms my heart;
>   awakens my mind
>   and speaks to my soul
>   in the universal language
>   of tones, semi-tones and velocities.

I lay myself down
>   on this deep blue purple carpet
>   of musical notes;
>   and slowly,
>   ever so slowly ...
>   I become the song.

Deep In The Shadows

Deep in the shadows of the vines,
      where waterfalls whisper and hide,
far away from beaches and waves
      remaining untouched by time and tide.

In a heavenly symphony of sound
      the sky, in wind-speak, talks to the trees.
Their roots carry messages underground
      as branches flutter and sway in the breeze.

Deep in the shadows of my mind
      I lie in the lap of music and song
where memories and dreams intertwine

      And I know this is where I belong ...
        inside the song in the song.

Dockside At Midnight

Ekphrastic poem written to the painting by Purple Flame
(Hermine Weiss & Candice James)

Look at the painting
and let your mind wander
the shorelines of imagination.

If you listen closely you'll hear it.
  The music of the wind,
the soft swish of the water,
the haunting whisper in the sky
and an atmosphere at home
within this symphony of silence;
anchored dockside with the boat
on this lake of midnight dreams
and music of the stars.

If you look closely you'll see it.

The moonbeams
polishing the trees with droplets of gold,
shining the water's obsidian gloss,
waltzing in sync with the sway of the boat,
reflecting deep in the depth of the scene
with the coveted promises
of what dreams may come.

Dockside at midnight ...
where dreams are born.

The Gathering Of The Trees

In the gathering of the trees
I romance the tears of an old June moon
      to coax dead memories to come alive.

Just beyond the Poplars,
      underneath the Elms,
            a ring of bright water and sparkling stars
      are creating a beautiful melody
that rises in torrid notes
      to dry the tears of the old June moon.

There is a clearing in a channel of the sky
      and a nearing in the stardust on high
            as I rest in the gathering of the trees
      in the midst of old June moon memories.

The ring of bright water and sparkling stars
      pull me into their magic
            and the whisper of your voice
      tugs at my heart
            and sings me back home again.

The Gold Of That Moment

Silvering down to a tarnished shine
I keep searching for the gold of that moment
we shared on yesterday's beach of dreams,
as we watched the sun dancing with diamonds
on the bright sparkling waters at Crescent Beach.

A throng of seagulls salted the sky
weaving in and out of the multi-colored kites
flying high on the edge of a sigh,
gliding with grace on the lip of the breeze.

I still hear your laughter warming my heart,
still feel your embrace warming my soul
as you swept the sea up into your eyes
in the gold of that moment so long ago.

Sometimes at night, in summertime dreams,
I wander yesterday's shorelines again.
On cool July days and hot August nights
the song of those days still plays in soft tones,
and inside the sweet ... your voice's refrain.

In the wake of reality's breaking dawn
the dream and my heart crack once again
the days of you and I are gone
and yesterday's wine is a fading pink stain.

On the cutting room floor of my memory
I keep searching for the special film clip
that spliced us together on yesterday's beach
in the heat of our youth and the gold of that moment ...

but the gold of that moment won't come again.

In The Amber Glow

The pale fading sky
longs for old violin strings
and the brush of a dusty bow
to compose a melody
that burns a bluer shade of amber
in the burnished orange embers
that still flicker in the ether.

This visual, staining my soul,
vibrates with a stir of echoes
that travel the canyons of my mind
in search of old strings
to hang a song high.

High enough to serenade the stars
and shine them
a bluer shade of gold
in the amber glow.

Sea Of Regret

Life plods on, day by day,
    like a sad song
on a broken sea of regret.

And the nights,
    the long, lonely nights,
are a never-ending,
      melancholy, suspended chord.

Background voices fade in ...
    then I hear a familiar voice.

Background music is hazy ...
    then I hear a familiar song
        singing me forward
    then back
into my long-lost years.

I see myself as a small cabin
    surrounded by a moat of my own making.

Too lonely too long,
I set sail in my barnacled ship
      on a static sea of silence
    searching for the song I lost,
      searching for the music
        that once was my soul ...
      searching,
  searching ...
      for the music
        and you.

Shuffle

You stiffened
       inside the liquid atmosphere of the dance
       and shuffled to the uneven beat of my heart.

       Your hand caressed the invisible tattoo
         you sewed to the cloth of my soul.
     You sketched me in shades of sepia
        and painted me in tones of blue
        and you thought you knew me well.

       I have been 33 shades of fog
         layered and woven
            into a fading rain.

    Wet with the tears
       of an unfinished song
       on the slippery dance floor of love
I stiffen inside the forgotten notes I lost

     .

A cherished memory turns cold
       in the heat of another lonely night
          and you shuffle
        to the uneven beat of my heart ...
          no more.

Summer In Your Hair

On a far and distant horizon
where the sun kneels down to the sea
I watched your eyes close over love
as you walked away from me.

Today inside my fading shadow
I dance to broken musical scores
trying to find the long-lost key
to open locked and fragile doors.

Questing and riding on whispering tides
tomorrow I'll set sail anew
searching for that lost horizon
and the old gold days of me and you.

If love is kind you'll still be there
with summer glistening in your hair.

The Waters Of Sleep

Descending into sleep
     in the embrace of soft music
         I begin to wander
     the dark velvet meadowlands of night.

I ride the consummate coat-tails
     of the music.
         It continues to compose itself
     as I slide into the glove
         of the dream chasing me.

     Hand on heart
         and palm in glove
     I fall through the music
         into the comforting waves
     and the tranquil waters of sleep.

Time Interrupted

Beneath a fading sky
in the twilight glitter
    of impending night,
        we fed the swans at dusk
    as the trees whispered secrets to us
    in the lush of the green divide.

    In the tangled brush of a kiss
        we danced
    in the tango of time interrupted.

And then the swans were swimming away
    as the stars crept in:
        one by one,
        two by two,
      and then a million more.

I'll always remember
    when we fed the swans at dusk
    in that blessed green divide
      before time interrupted
        and sliced us
      into separate lives;
and we danced away from each other
    in the tangled tango
      of timeless time.

Winter's Thin Pines

The wind ruffles the pale sheets
of dusk's frail silhouette
as it hobbles, in a stumbling, ghostly gait,
down wet October streets.

A bevy of discarded candy wrappers
dance haphazardly across
an abandoned carnival shadowland,
adrift on a field of dreams.

Frost gathers on the horizon,
as November awakens and rises
to the sound of distant grand piano
playing broken chords and errant notes
in a neglected unfinished song.

Then, suddenly the music stops.
December arrives with no ticket to ride
and no plans for the future.

Between the thin pines
dusk shatters and scatters
into the bruised arms
of a wandering twilight.

I sit down at the piano,
play a sad, sad song,
think on days gone by
and your frail silhouette disappearing
into the deep of winter's shadowland..

Beautiful Magic

You come to me softly in dreams every night
inside its citadel holding me tight
at the edge of a broken twilight dawn
where everything but the dream is gone.

The orchestra's tuned for a rock symphony
I'm writing this song to you from me.
and all my days bittersweet and tragic
are blown away in this beautiful magic

A new day is dawning. I cling to the shine
swaying and dancing on its quarter line.
We're chasing our shadows outrunning the sun
into the moonlight coming undone.

The orchestra's tuned for a symphony
in a classical retrograde melody
and all my days bittersweet and tragic
are blown away in this beautiful magic

I'm balancing deftly on high wires and rope.
Dangling loosely on the frayed edge of hope.
There's a taste to the air not there before
leaving me hungrier and wanting more.

And all my days bittersweet and tragic
are blown away in this beautiful magic.
Just blown away
in this beautiful magic.

A Distant Moaning

A distant moaning:
a silent song, a wordless rhyme,
drums whispering a broken lullaby beat.
The dead dance to their own music.
They dance to the songs only they can hear.

A string of pearls.
A chain of golden silver.
A pendant of burnt amber.
A candle of sage and sienna.

These are the things
that remind me of the dead.
These are the things I will take to the dance
when I hear the distant moaning
and move slowly across
Time's river of tears
toward the dance of the dead.

Forever ... Yet Never

There's a sweet, heavy thrill
moving through the atmosphere;
              a staccato jazz note
                skipping magnetism's rope.

Eyes across a crowded room meet
         genuflecting fire as they linger
               locked in the moment.

Strangers in most ways
       but the music within
            recognizes the rhythm
     of the familiar heartbeat
moving through the atmosphere:
       electrifying the moment,
           stretching it to infinity,
     an everlasting pull
through the center of the music,
     the truth of the song
        resonating
   as the lovers move toward each other
        unraveling themselves
   into the new composition
       they are creating
           from moments long ago;
      lifetimes ago
   to live in each other again
suspending the jazz chord they are
    forever ... yet never.

The Only Moment

The first time I saw you
      you seemed familiar.
            The more I looked at you
      the more I wanted you.

So far away in mind and body
      but so connected
            in spirit and soul.

      And the music played.

A few times in the same room
      miles apart in body
            moving closer in soul
      we kept locking eyes
            and unlocking the past.

Then one time, suddenly,
      across the table
            you were sitting there.
            So close. Looking at me

      And the music played

I was swept away
            in the beat of your heart
      and the rhythm of the moment.

The only moment that ever mattered.
  The only moment that ever will.

Raw Red Nightmare

Each dance step I take
proves a clumsy experiment.
Falling over the moon.
Drowned on the shores of Tripoli.

I watch you from my barstool
parading your expertise
inside a spotlight tango.

Applauding too hard I slip from my chair
and see myself fall from your grace.

Your face doesn't bless me
nor do your fingers
as I grasp for a thread from your heart.

I release my vice grip
and see my weakened thread
reverberating in slow motion fade out
inside a tender waltz
        turned harsh.

Tumbling Down

Shakespeare said it with quill and ink
and inspiration's golden link
and the words came tumbling down:
In sonnets and verses, plays and prose.
In theatres, and travelling minstrel shows.
His passion still rages and spills from the pages
onto the glitter of sound sets and stages.
Tumbling down ... still tumbling down.

Mozart said it with notes and keys
in compositions and symphonies
and the music came tumbling down:
Illuminating the darkness undressing.
Devils, angels and lovers confessing.
The agonies and ecstasies.
In serenades and rhapsodies.
Tumbling down ... still tumbling down.

Michelangelo said it with paints and brush
guided by an angel's touch
and the colours came tumbling down:
To halo the Sistine Chapel's ceiling
With Saints, cherubs, and angels kneeling.
A masterpiece of holiness.
Saving Grace and forgiveness.
Tumbling down ... still tumbling down.

Artists, Musicians, Poets and Sages.
Droplets of gold on history's pages.
Tumbling down throughout the ages.
Their world of beauty surrounds us still.
Their legacy is a living will.
Tumbling down ... forever tumbling down.

.

Author Profile

Candice James, is a professional writer, poet, visual artist, musician, singer/songwriter, workshop facilitator and book reviewer for a variety of Publishing Houses, Canadian Poetry Review and Pacific Rim Review of Books. She completed her 2nd three year term as Poet Laureate of The City of New Westminster, BC CANADA in June 2016 and was appointed Poet Laureate Emerita in November 2016 by order of City Council. Her credentials are: Founder of: Poetry New Westminster; Fred Cogswell Award For Excellence In Poetry; Poetry In The Park; Poetic Justice, Slam Central; Royal City Literary Arts Society; Past President of Royal City Literary Arts Society; Past President of Federation of British Columbia Writers; and Past Director of SpoCan. She has been keynote speaker at "Word On The Street", "Black Dot Roots Cultural Collective", "Write On The Beach"; "Dialogue on Death and Dying" and she has been a judge for the League of Canadian Poets "Pat Lowther Memorial Award" and "Jessamy Stursberg Youth Poet Award" and has also judged The Fred Cogswell Award". She received Pandora's Collective Vancouver Citizenship Award; and the Bernie Legge Artist/Cultural award.

Candice has featured at many venues both civic and public and appeared on television and radio. She has presented workshops, mentored writers; written prefaces and reviews, published articles, and short stories. Her poetry has been translated into Arabic, Italian, German, Bengali Chinese, and Farsi. Her artwork has appeared in Duende Magazine and "Spotlight" Goddard College of Fine Arts, (Vermont, USA) and her poetry has appeared in and artwork "Unmasked" on the cover of Survision Magazine, (Dublin, Ireland) and her poetry and artwork have appeared in Wax Poetry Art Magazine Canada.

Website www.candicejames.com
YouTube
https://www.youtube.com/channel/UC2EA5GcECIGYuF3o2K KHJFQ

FACEBOOK
https://www.facebook.com/search/top?q=candice%20james%20-%20poet%20laureate%20emerita
ARTIST
https://www.facebook.com/CandiceJamesArtist?fref=ts

MUSICIAN-
https://www.facebook.com/pages/Candice-James-Songwriter-Bass-Guitarist/156859754352277?fref=ts

SOUND CLOUD –
https://soundcloud.com/user-45844113

TWITTER-
@NWPoLoEmerita
        and
@candice23809987